Soul Shards

by Del Thoreau

Published by Existence Publishing, Delphine Thoreau
61 rue de Lyon, 75012 Paris France
Cover and illustrations designed by Del Thoreau

ISBN: 978-2-9590256-2-4

To my family,
Who has always been there for me,

To Athénaïs, Cécile, Manon and Marie,
For having been another family for so many years,

To Minolie,
For making me a better writer, for being one of my closest friends, for being a partner in crime,

To Αθηνά,
For being such a loving warmth in my life, for being my loudest cheerleader and precious little treasure,

To Siska,
For being such an incredibly important part of my life, particularly my creative life.

To the people I have loved and hated,
Whom have inspired so many of my poems.

Table of Contents

Author's Note

Obscurité contains poems dealing with mental health.
Red District contains poems dealing with sexuality.

WORDS ARE LIKE NEURONS AND GRAVITY,
THEY CONNECT US ALL

Stardust

All of us are star stuff, born of stardust,
Created as one on this planet's crust;
Amidst the rest, here you are,
A pure note in the universe's symphony,
A vibration,
That calls to me, that calls to me.
Our worldlines bright with energy, curving
The very fabric of spacetime,
Will they converge? Will you be mine?
Unique expression of a whole,
Thoughts spiraling into their own black hole,
A look in the starry night of your gaze
Suffice to pull me through the craze.
It's dark out there and obscure,
So I gravitate to you,
My galaxy, my wonder, so pure.

Sapphic Thoughts

Useless Defense

I'm scared, and I should hide away and run to the other side,
Because I fear that my heart might get stolen, crushed,
turned to dust,
And I can still feel it beating, loud, hard, frantic inside,
It never stops, alongside yours, from the brightest dawn to the
darkest dusk.
Sat here, with just pen and ink to warm my soul, to bleed,
I try to remember when was planted in me such a powerful seed,
And I pour my thoughts into words, disjointed, raw, and
unrefined,
To keep you at bay, to push you away so you could leave my
mind.
But the more I write, the more your presence solidifies;
How could I think it would make you go away?
And the more I burn, the more I wish my love would turn to ice.

A Certain Flutter

There is a trembling that I can't stop,
A flutter somewhere, the sour taste of hope,
That was ignited by this star I dare not touch,
Too far down, how could I think I was able to do such.
There is this restlessness of the mind,
At the thought of you, at the thought of you,
That looking elsewhere doesn't seem to halt,
What should I do, oh please, what should I do?
Ghost memories, golden fantasies
Just keep haunting all those moments, all those places.
Reprieve for the exhausted, pleas from the hurt,
Just leave, abandon this dreamland expert.

Heartstrings

My heart sings in the soft light of the setting sun,
As you stroke its strings like a guitar, you make me feel
A thousand things I thought I had forgotten,
And every one of your thoughts is a petal I love to steal.
I forget the tears, I forget the depth of the ocean I loved to drown in,
I just stand on the warm sand of your words, the waves I watch
Remind me of the ripples you've made on my mind that's been healing;
It feels like falling, endlessly, and for once, I wish there was no catch.
I forget the hours that drift away as I wander on this path with you
Hidden in the forest of our past, of secrets shared, of treasures found,
And my head is full of your laughter, of your smile, even without any sound.

Wave

Like a wave, we flow in and out of existence,
Rising above all for a short period of time,
Between ups and downs, a perpetual dance
To the song of the sublime.
The way you love me is like a wave
That I sometimes surf to my greatest ecstasy,
Or that I chase incessantly
As you abandon me right when I crave.
Your power upon me like the primordial waters,
I come running to the snap of your fingers.
Your absence an abyss I can never get used to
As you come back right when I forget you.
And it comes back to rolling hips like rolling seas,
Desire flowing like sea foam soaking up soil,
Until you leave me as I try to reach for the sublime
To rot in cold, sticky grime.

You Exist Everywhere

You feel like a cup of coffee in the morning at dawn,
Like a cup of tea warming my hands in the twilight.
I see you in the soft purple of the sky at the rise of the sun,
In the copper hue shining through my windows from the sunset light.
You feel like a nap by the river in the soft breeze, music in my ears,
Like being awake in the darkest hours of the night, the complete silence,
I hear you in the soft notes of music, twirling my soul through a slow dance,
I hear you in those singers' desperate, scorched voice, those tears.
You feel like the secret I wouldn't share, too intimate,
You feel like the name I want to shout at the sky,
You feel like the first thought in the morning, the last before sleep.
I feel like a maze with a design, a path to my heart so intricate,
I feel like a passionate ambition-filled lover that would die,
I feel like, for you, with you, because of you, I could fall so deep.

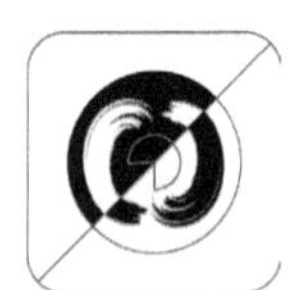

Roses

For you, a garden of red roses,
Red roses for the passion in my veins,
Thorns for the distance that causes pain,
For you, a garden of red roses.
A single white rose on your bed,
A white rose for the pure love I have for thee,
One flower for the lover I long to see,
A single white rose on your bed.
One key in my hand,
Cold like nights without you,
One key in my hand,
For the door that leads to you.

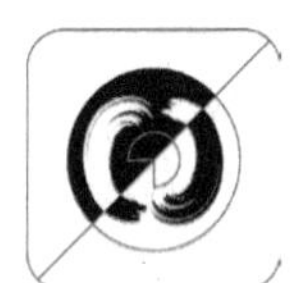

Nest

You've made yourself a little nest in the center of my heart,
Lighting a steady fire that warms me whole,
Creating shadows of a beauty I had never seen,
And through your eyes, I'm so beautiful, it seems.
And for now, it feels like we could never be concrete,
Like the universe is keeping us apart,
But as I'll travel the world through the years, from the start,
I'll do it to bring the world to you bit by bit.
You're like the breath of life that strengthens and steadies my every move,
Taking my soul by the hand and dragging it from the night,
Giving it a hunger for life, for the light,
That I had lost somewhere along with my groove.

Pile of Rubble

I was stumbling, carrying all the pieces of my broken heart in my arms.
Some spill, and I trip over them,
Sometimes I fall to my knees, and they all scatter around,
And I'm left there to pick them up for such a long while,
Those heavy pieces with their dim light flickering out.
One day, our paths crossed, and you became a shelter.
I left my heart at the door, in a pile of rubble.
Finally able to lose myself in someone's arms,
I left the flames lick my whole being over and over...
And I couldn't tell you if the burns hurt; all I did was contemplate
Those scars covering my body.
Sometimes we would have reprieves from the scorching passion
And your caresses would heal me for a brief moment, reprieve.
But you invited my broken heart inside...
As days went by, you stole every piece of it,
Broken piece by broken piece,
It still lies in a pale pile of rubble,
Yet somehow, its burden is no longer so heavy.

Forbidden Soulmates

Soulmates, I feel your name in my heartbeat,
Found you when I was hunched over on the concrete.
A sobbing mess in a pile of heart pieces,
Shattered, scattered, there were so many bruises.
I was looking for a drug, a medicine for my pains,
So I pumped your sweet, addictive words into my veins.
Looking for a reprieve, lust-filled distractions,
All I found was a new painful addiction.
Laughing like a madwoman, I opened myself up,
Exposing my naked soul so it could be beaten up.
I plunged headfirst to get a dizzy mind,
To forget for a while, so I didn't have to be kind.
Laying naked on my heart's tombstone,
High on sex, your domination had me stoned,
My body moving to your filthy words,
Drooling like one of your depraved whores.
Forbidden soulmates, the Universe separates us,
And all my stitched-up heart can do is leak pus.
So we're traveling on parallel paths, fingertips touching,
I ache: our roads are never crossing.
I smile when you say you want me to be someone else's,
I nod and agree so you won't see me heartbroken, hopeless.
You want us weak so our bond doesn't strengthen,
When I want it indestructible, you see it barren.
I want it eternal, but you rub it off like chalk.
And I'm supposed to witness this and not bawl?!
But hey,
Illuminated by the same sun, we aren't too far apart,
I stand in the shade, over before we even start,
But hey,
I still let you hold my bleeding heart in your hands,
Lone tears and a smile and my world's once again bland.
Poetry's begging to be made for you,
And yet I can't find the words
That would be precisely right,
To describe my love for you.

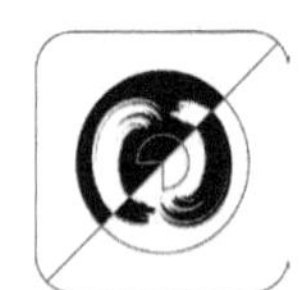

Specters and Fading Memories

Our future splits into two paths, each filled with thorns, breaking my heart.
So I turn a blind eye, turn my back to tomorrow, and choose to lose myself in the now.
We whisper passion-filled promises, anguished pleas, and feverish vows,
Just to forget for a moment, just a fleeting while, the road ahead that parts.
Fingers cramping up, trembling from holding on too hard to the here, to the present,
My smile, tainted by my unshed tears, imprisons a strangled sob.
All I want to feel is your arms holding me tight, my senses surrounded by your scent,
But my heart is ripped from my chest, broken, wailing in a last painful throb.
In the dead of night, with your body pressed to mine, an arm around my waist,
I lay awake, eyes staring at the dark wall, seeing myself all alone, on my knees,
Wrecked and tear-stained, having naught but the ghost of your embrace
And of a time when I'd drown in your kisses: specters and fading memories.

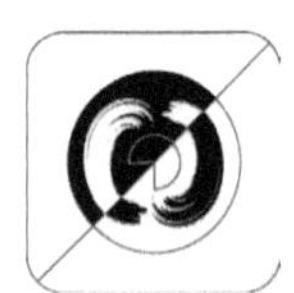

Emotional Masochist

It was the easiest thing, falling for you
But you made it so hard it stings,
Loving you.
I want to be yours forever,
I want, and I want, and I break with every beat.
I'm an emotional masochist, offering you my heart,
Blood splatters around like some twisted kind of art,
You are like a surgery with opened chest;
Seducing me like you're on some kind of quest.
Please don't leave me in the middle of a storm
That will turn everything around me to dust.
You used to make me feel so seen,
But now I'm living like Mrs Invisible.

Not Mine To Hold

Meeting a fascinating soul that speaks to me, mine latches onto it,
And I keep drinking it in, and drinking it in until it dries up and becomes boring,
So dull that in my arrogance, I turn away, so stupid, so fucking undeserving,
And my soul drags my heart through the mud, leashed, behaving as it sees fit.
And I hate it. I hate myself for wanting you, for needing you, for thinking you're mine,
Mine to adore, mine to cherish, mine to consume, and absorb and dispose
As I lose interest and turn away, leaving you cold, walking away and shredding my heart 'cause
I couldn't bear the thought of you away, so free when I was encaged by your essence so divine.
And I'm trying to outrun time when I know I'll lose you; I try to hold back those feelings bottled up,
And I hold onto each memory, never letting go; I hold onto every word, never letting myself forget,
Because the moment I do is the moment you'll be gone, from my heart, from my life, and upset,
I could scratch every layer off my being, reaching for the wretched, the rotten, the very core that hurts.
But don't you ever think for a moment that I was never consumed with love, with passion, with adoration
For everything that you were, everything that you are and could be,
But in my desperation for a world where my feelings reined free, storming with need, clouded by lust, alit by attraction,
I forgot that you weren't mine to have, never could, and my heart longs to be free.

Still

I happened to look up at the sky, tonight;
Piercing through the darkness, there was the moon, o so bright,
And as I stared at its soothing glow dreamingly,
You once again appeared before me, o so clearly.
Why can't my heart move on and let go,
When I know there could be no hope
Of my unrequited love being shared,
Must I still cry to myself to bed?
Just when I think I'm cured, it comes back again,
With a single smile of yours imprinting in my brain
Setting on fire my whole being,
Blowing alive the candle of my passion, now a great burning.
All my heart needs to long for you once more
Is just a look from your eyes, piercing through my soul,
And when whatever inch of your body moves,
I just keep watching, in a trance, intense blues.
But still, after all these years, I still wonder,
To curse or to bless this feeling, I still ponder,
Cause, after all, you still bring me happiness, love,
A force with which I temporarily rise above.
May it be the joy or the pain, do I truly care?
For when I'm feeling all of this, I feel alive, I dare,
And when it seems to drift away, I mourn,
And agonizing, I happen to look up at the moon.

Broken Heart

We've been having this dance for so long now,
Creating a web around us,
I'm trapped though I've never felt more free
Than lying in your arms.
Why is it so hard, looking back on past lives,
Choking on tears that I thought had dried.
Why were you such a perfect match,
Lighting up my life, my days?
Why did things change so fast,
And colored everything back to grey?
I was so used to this,
Being the woman you were running to,
And I don't recognize this,
Us,
I am lost in something new.
I felt like I could be myself, never hide anything.
Thank you for never judging who I am.
Words have never flowed more freely,
With you, I felt like I could be me.
The universe snatched it away,
And I'm left wandering in a broken heart,
In a tormented mind,
Wondering when I fell this hard for you,
If I'd change it if back then I knew.

My Fix

Used and abused
My heart's left bruised.
You got me my fix, addicted, intoxicated,
And I crawl back every time.
To get my fix, I take it all in, the bad.
I see what you're doing,
But your words are so addicting.
You gave me all I need.
Charmed me.
God, you're oh so charming.
You whisper everything I want to hear.
And I crawl back to you for my easy fix.
Wanting to heal my broken heart,
I let you twist your knife in the wounds instead.
It feels so good to sin, to defile and abandon myself
In your fake safety.
I know the pain it causes,
And I crawl back to get my fix.
I'm addicted to you, in love with your words,
Even through my tears, vision blurred.
I let you break me some more,
A thousand pieces.
You took away my fix, and I'm still begging, still crawling.
I'm in love with your words,
Even when you help my demons rise.
You toy with me,
I know you do.
So I whore myself out,
Whore my heart out,
And I still crawl back to you.

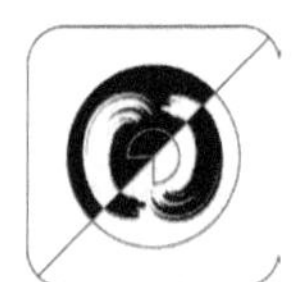

Breakup

You made me feel special... desirable.
With you, I felt I could belong.
The darkest, dirtiest parts of my heart were matched,
Or so it seemed...
All of me was loved and wanted,
Free to be who I am.
As a result, my heart opened and grew.
I let it all out, my love, my burning desires. For you.
They got bigger, stronger every day.
Until you turned away.
Slowly, your doors closed, and I was left watching, powerless.
I was naked, facing walls –taller every day.
Exposed and overflowing with an orphaned need, it drowned me.
Tears fell as we talked and talked about this, relentlessly,
About you not desiring me. Not anymore. Did you ever?
I would cry my heart out, cut off from what made me whole.
I forced myself to accept this, to live with only memories of open arms.
Slowly, my desires withdrew, tired of being repressed and pushed down.
They disappeared.
My body, once vibrating with life, boiling with lust,
Turned to stone, cold and dead.
At least I still had the sun of your love.
Until you turned away.
My heart had already shut you out, silently, over the months,
Exhausted from the growing distance.
So it hurt less, I guess,
When you told me you didn't love me,
Not anymore. Did you ever?
What hurts the most, my love, is that you don't know if you ever did.

Without Your Gaze

I feel broken inside, without your gaze,
I know I shouldn't, standing on my own two feet,
Nothing no more that would amaze
This frozen shell on an empty cliff.
A thousand worlds, a thousand words,
That meant everything to me,
Now hollow and shallow birds
That sing my floating away, the deepest sea.
The needed ghost of your arms around me,
The distant memory of a voice,
The longing need for me to see
That you're too here to be a choice.
In the mirror, I stare back at two black eyes,
Familiar yet never the same, always insane,
And my heart tugs, painful thuds, and tries
To remember the taste of your name.

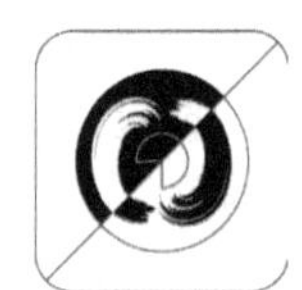

Shredded Heart

A shredded heart, you left me with a shredded heart,
One that hurts with every beat, that struggles to play the part.
I sit here, thinking back to us, the love so warm, innocence
That didn't survive.
Maybe it just wasn't meant to, but the memories fade,
The way you smiled, your smell, your embrace.
Those endless words have become so sparse.
Why?
Are they now someone else's?
They will never taste the same; we will never be the same.
Did we disappear? Who we were.
We came as one to create a unique flavor, a secret color;
Now the past fades to grey, the world's lost your shade
And my heart still breaks every now and then,
There are still a few tears that I shed.
My love turned to a whisper that I will have to learn to live with.
Sometimes it's hard, when I think too much, when I feel too
much,
Our love an old, tarnished photograph.
I loved to see myself through your eyes
Because I am blind.
You didn't hurt me, and yet
All the parts I disrobed to you, I now hide even more,
Were they meant only for you?
A shredded heart, you left me with a shredded heart,
One that forgot, now scared to play its natural part.

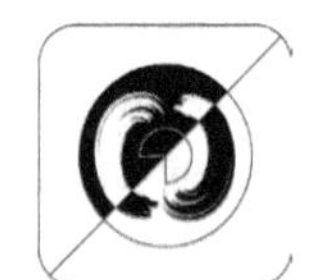

Keeping You Here

It's been years since you've been gone.
And every morning, I whisper your name to the morning sky.
And every night, I talk to your pillow, alone.
I laugh during the day to hide that at night, I still cry.
I hold on to the memory of you, to keep you immortal.
I reject the living, not to diminish your home in my heart.
And I keep writing for you, turn your soul into art,
If I love again, will you disappear? Would it be a betrayal?
I do not want to live if you can't; how is it fair?
I do not want to love if it's not you, not even care.
Every little act meant to keep you there,
Every thought meant to keep you here.
What if our love can only live through me?
If I move on, will it have ever existed?
I hurt, without you, without us, so deeply,
On certain days, I just wait to be departed.

I Wonder

Do you still think about me sometimes?
Do I ever cross your mind?
Because you do mine,
And I always wonder...
How is it that I lost you so?
You were never someone that I wished drifted away,
And yet here we are,
And I don't know what to say.
Is it so painful to stay by my side?
Am I the problem?
Or just never good enough to be kept.
I don't like it,
Being invisible to your heart,
Because you're still crystal clear
In mine.
Do you still think about me sometimes?
Do I ever cross your mind?

Indulge

In this spring morning's warmth, let me indulge a little
In a dance to the sound of your voice
Let me smile with my eyes, steal from me a soft giggle,
Embracing life like I have no choice.
In this summer's early afternoon, let me indulge, will you,
In a nap under a tree's foliage that dances in the breeze,
Laughing while lying on the grass, fingers grazing –what a tease,
As we imagine a life together, as if our love was true.
In this autumn's sunset, let me indulge, for a while,
In the hope that you'll remain in my arms by the fire,
As we sit in peaceful silence, staring at the flames,
Though I know that things will never be the same.
In this winter's lonely night, let me indulge, for once,
In the tears that warm my skin
As I grieve under a heavy blanket of what once was,
What was too beautiful to be a sin.

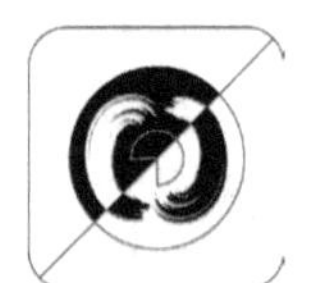

Darlingest

You grace my thoughts lately,
(More than you have for years)
Haunting my heart tirelessly,
(Ghosts of what were not, ghosts of what could have been.)
I find myself crashing our secret place,
Curled up on the couch, tears down my face,
As I lay motionless, draped in memories
Of tender affection and unsung pleas.
In the dead of night, darlingest,
Your lips still claim mine...
(I find myself longing for them best.)
The phantom touch of our hours-long embrace
Igniting a fire - it still warms me to this day.
Regrets of breaking your heart and silencing mine.
Will you hold this piece of me?
(For yet a little while.)

Coming Home

Blood dripping, painting the earth, echoing in the silence,
Tears rolling down, quenching my heart's thirst, penance,
Dirt on my clothes, on my shoes, from the endless roads
That, until in your arms I collapse, I will still roam.
Exhaustion wearing me down, harsh and persistent,
Sweat covering me like a second skin, protecting,
I'll have wandered the world and countless seas,
Just to come home, to your eyes, to your melodies.
I'll come bearing the gifts of a thousand winds, a thousand leaves,
An infinity of landscapes in my eyes, always leading to you,
As all those out there dream of clouds, of sinking treasures, mysteries,
I've done it all, and nothing holds in life a more precious place than you.

A New Definition

I used to believe love to be those burning fires, those raging feelings, and torments,
I used to believe it was all about those scorched lovers, bloodied and full of scars,
That it was poems ripped right from the heart, shouted at the moon, at the stars,
And restless nights, daydreams, a head full of desires; a full life now turned crescent.
But with you, I know it's about the secret smiles from wordless gazes,
I know it's also tender touches just to know you are here, a fleeting always.
Your arms around me, a warm embrace, like a summer sun, a Sunday morning,
And those dreams, your vision, your thoughts, all whispered but so inspiring.
The poet in me will keep being transcended by this otherworldly passion,
Sparked by the warmth you bathe my heart in, by the love in your eyes.
She will still wish to lay down words, so devastating, enraptured, chained,
Like savage wolves howling at the night sun, tearing apart all that I am, destruction,
To honor, to tell the tales of the simplicity, the ease, the serenity that inspires
The woman I love so wholly, so holy, sharing a feeling so pure it can't be claimed.

Reason

Won't you be the reason for my smile?
Won't you be the reason why I forget it all for a little while?
I look at you with stars in my eyes;
Won't you take me with you, spending life soaring through the skies?
Just give me a reason to believe, a reason for hope to bloom
In my heart; with you, days slow down and never end too soon.
I wander along a path of swaying flowers, a silly smile on my lips,
So what if you make me feel like the silly girl I am?
Look what a giddy mess you turned me into, happiness spills.
You tuck my hair behind my ear, and I blush, "Just scram!"
I do not want to reason with the rhythm in my chest.
In my life, my home, my heart, you'll always be a guest.
Safe in your embrace, I dream of walks and journeys around the globe,
Holding your hand, laughter swirling all around, wearing love as robes.
Let me just nuzzle your neck and hum, content
As I'm brought home by your familiar scent.
I do not need to reason, I do not need a reason, love in the air,
It's enough, just hold me tight, I have enough love to spare.

Intensity

Is that where all the answers are kept?
In the intensity of your gaze?
In what you whisper to me in the dead of the night?
When it gets too much, and my chest gets too tight.
A condensed bubble of space-time,
A con of a dance in the springtime
Is what it feels to me, this intensity.
Why turn your attention to me?
Therein lies all the answers, I guess,
Not in the subject of your search, mind you,
But in the laser-sharp focus of consciousness
That pierces the intangible to see what's true.

Loving Her

She felt like fate put in motion, life laying her in my arms.
She was a treasure I had never thought to search for.
Gentle smiles in the loneliest hour of the night, at four,
The stars swimming in her eyes, they all always made me warm.
It was in the comfort of the book in her hands as she sat next to me,
It was in her hand on the small of my back as she walked past,
Soft footsteps on the floor in the morning, loving gazes at breakfast,
The lazy cuddles and bright giggles that she readily offered me.
Long conversations existed in a second-lasting glance,
Like promises in the corner of her lips as she smirked at dusk,
Thousands of stories played out in her embrace, in a dance,
And when she laughed, head tilted back, she became my luck.
Her love was like road trips in the middle of the night, windows rolled down,
It was like petals falling from the trees and floating in the wind,
Loving her was the silence after confessions, the space between words,
It was as simple as a breath, as easy as a daydream, and just as devastating.

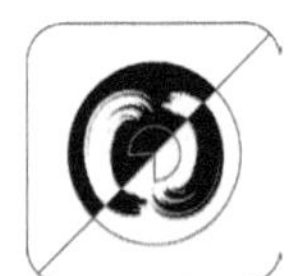

Texture

There are particular things that I rejoice in.
The feeling of fresh sheets on my bathed skin,
The bumps of veins under my fingertips,
The grass tingling my palms, your kiss on my lips.
Because, you see, it's all in the textures,
The sensations I hunt down like a vulture.
It's finding the divine through your hand in mine,
Your touch gently running through my hair,
Your heartbeat against my cheek as I stare.
My only hope, darling, is to experience the feeling
Of your skin going from soft to wrinkling.

Obscurité

Loss

Maddening, your world can shatter so suddenly,
Warm laughter on a summer night by silence replaced...
Dissonance in the distance, no thoughts, vision blurry,
Left alone facing the truth, no choice but to be afraid.
How to find meaning when love can disappear in a blink of an eye?
Scoffing at the creeping pain, looking up at the infinity beyond, at the sky,
Looking for answers, thoughts, and memories thrown lose inside,
Everything to keep them near, just a moment still, ‘til the pain subsides.
Anger may rise from time to time, like a shield to a mourning soul,
A blanket of white-hot fury to burn away the numbing cold,
But colors will pop back from all the grey, over time,
Hands reaching for you through the dark, breathing lifeline.
Lost forever but ever-present all the same,
In all you are, all you will live, without a name,
Living through you, memories, and smiles.
From the past guiding your every step,
Their love propelling you forward, no missteps,
They'll be walking beside you for a while.

Behind a Wall of Steel

Lost, everything dark and blurry around me, swirling and shouting,
All I feel is a connection, deep, like a lifeline to keep hoping,
But it burns, freezes, soft and harsh, punishing, tearing me apart,
Potential, stupid imagination – was it like this at the start?
My blood is crimson, thick – I want it ink and paint,
Arrogance, and it hurts so bad when I can't feel
What used to make me suffer and create, a martyr, a saint,
Now emotions reined in, chained, unruly behind a wall of steel.
Jealousy, need, a desire to break free, all leashed to my heart but still struggling;
Love, happiness, lust, radiating freely, untamed, raw, and pulsating;
Pain, burning rage, and loneliness sometimes creeping up from the shadows.
Good girl, bad girl, untamed yet unrevealed, feelings chained up effortlessly so,
My body craving, moving, living of its own accord, demanding, consumed
As my mind wanders, lives a thousand lives, feels and just assumed.

Quarantine

During these times of quarantine, I have seen it all,
The good in people that will help and support at the desperate call
While the bad in others whispers a search for riches and power
At the cost of the lives and the well-being of their brother.
And at the end of each day rains a new number
Like Death coming to gloat on teleprompters
Of the number of cases, the number of deceased
Of each country... a macabre race... may it cease!
And every night, anxiety seizes me, back from her grave,
Making me worried and afraid as I'm trying to stay brave.
Every morning comes as a blessing, filled with too much to do,
See, I do it all because what if tomorrow I'm dying too?
But tonight, the Moon hangs full like an expecting Mother,
Maybe she'll birth hope and healing to the world,
So I'll pray, in the dead of the night, in my whispers to her
That tomorrow comes, alive with her light, letting everything unfurl.

Syndrome

It's like a disease that's never been heard of,
Words that I don't mean just shoot off,
Muscles seizing up in an uncontrollable rage,
There's nothing, it seems, that can assuage
The anger boiling and spreading all over
That covers my eyes and makes it all darker.
If a voice or a smile breaks through like sunlight
Through cloudy skies and mournful rains,
Then they appear like saccharine stains
And what should be my salvation becomes my blight.
Unknown to any scientist, this degenerate syndrome,
It'll plague me forevermore until I'm windblown.

Explosion

Oh, here's a new poem for you; I'll make it black as ink
And as violent as the anger running through my fucking veins.
The lack of respect from you is boiling my brain
With desires to make you suffer as much as I can think.
Shooting you in the face, beating your fucking face to a pulp
Anything so you close your goddamn mouth, making you whimper like a pup
I hate you, and I have for years; it really is hard to respect someone
That doesn't respect you back – your words irritating moans.
Fuck you and everything you think, everything you say,
I hate you so fucking much, and yet all my brain says
Is to punch a wall till my hands bleed,
Clench my jaw till my teeth shatter,
As if that would change anything,
As if it'd make things better.
Fuck you, it's you who built me up to think so low of myself,
Fuck you, it's you who has never been there,
I hate you and all you represent, fuck you, fuck you, fuck you.

My Prison

Walking around aimlessly, wandering in the dark
No matter how bright the sun can be these days,
I live in a prison that no one sees, and I feel stark.
Chains and bars stretching as far as the eye can see,
My cage isn't made of steel but of faraway ideals.
Living in obedience my whole life, without rebelling,
My prison stayed strong, good as new, unmoving,
And now that my soul starts fighting back,
Will I start my journey and pick up the slack?

Tonight

I'm all muddy tonight, and it's not rainy, and it's not dirty,
I feel alone; I'm alone. I'm lonely, lone, lonesome, and then some,
And my heart sinks and feels heavy, filled with lead and covered in leaves,
And I'm trying to be, and it feels like I don't know anymore.
Is anything worth it at all,
The trouble? The struggle?
The forever battle;
But you're my beacon, my light,
For me, who still stands in the cold, untouched by your warmth.
So far away, so far away, my dear,
And the darkness ebbs its way near;
You smell like spring on my cold winter nights,
A genuine smile in a grey crowd,
But tonight, I'm so far away, so far away, my dear,
So far inside.
Inside.
It's cold.
Lone.
Empty but filled 'till I choke.
Just a touch, just a voice, at the horizon,
My back turns, my stomach churns, my heart burns.
Blind. Mute. Worthless. Abandon.

Minefield

I walk on this path every day, minefield, mind filled
With worries and questions and desires, expression,
My body's buzzing, and I itch to break the wall,
But I crumble, standing tall, and I fall, and I fall.
Blind, I used to look, but now, for the first time, I see,
Paralyzed, I used to live in a cage, but now am I free?
I move, and I move, I dance, and I am, I feel,
Somehow my heart isn't always made of steel.
Body, mind, and soul so disconnected, lost at sea,
Drifting away, bathed in human, bathed in soiled,
I'm just yearning to breathe and cry and just be,
I want to expand and grow; never more will I recoil.

Horror

It doesn't have to be under the covet of the night for the worst feelings to come out.
It could be creeping up on me as the sun warms my face.
It slowly settles upon me, this heaviness of the heart and unshakable doubt,
When thoughts invade my head, saying this isn't my place.
Younger, I used to think that with more freedom, I would have it figured out...
But here I am, over a decade later, and it feels like I didn't even start...
I don't just feel out of place, I feel out of kin, just drifting away and apart,
Looking for people who would miss me and a life I could carve out.
At night those thoughts come in voices akin to demons and monsters assailing me,
But in the daylight, I realize, bittersweet, that those voices, well, they're just me.
Sometimes they make me want to scream until I cough up blood with no voice left,
Bashing my head against the wall until emptiness is the only thing left.
Sometimes the horror leaves, and I'm just left sitting there, staring into nothing.

Sweet Melody

I wander through the days in a haze,
Standing still where I used to run in haste,
The world's blurry and grey and worthless,
I'm so numb, bleeding, thank goodness.
My heart's a black hole, my mind a prison,
My demons standing behind laughing in abandon,
«We got you good. You thought you'd crawl out of this hole,
We got you good. We'll watch you grow cold,
Keep running, sweetheart, keep hoping,
We'll steal it all and watch you die, laughing.»
They stand in my shadow all day, growing taller as the sun sets,
Swallowing me whole with the night.
«No one likes you,
No one cares,
Everyone leaves,
You're worthless,
Motionless,
Look at you, ugly fat ass,
They don't care,
You don't care,
Stay down,
Lie still,
Just wait for death to spill.»
Their sweet melody, I know it by heart,
They swallow me whole, in my black hole heart.

Sometimes I Wish

Sometimes I wish I would cut myself open
Just to see if what they say is true,
To see if it gets it all out of me
All this darkness, this thickness inside.
Sometimes I wish I would do drugs
To see if what they say is true,
To see if it helps me escape
This reality I don't want to witness.
Sometimes I wish I would get black-out drunk
To see if what they say is true,
To see if it could help me forget
That I'm not where I want to be.
Yet I have no choice, I'm left here to endure
This life that weighs too much for my shoulders;
Yet I have no choice, I'm left here to live
Through those death wishes in this cold cage.
My cowardice, my fears holding me back
From being self-destructive as I sometimes dream,
And her sheer existence, the mere thought of her
Are enough to pull me off this storm, this alluring pit.

Self-Harm

You cut yourself to relieve the pain from your heart, your mind,
But you don't want it forever gone, you'd be blind,
So you engrave it on your body so it won't disappear...
What would become of you if pain were to leave?
The scars on your skin a reminder of your suffering,
Old wounds not to forget, old wounds to know you're still there,
And in a storm of thoughts, to fight the clutches of darkness, maddening,
You cut, you slice, you bleed as much as you can bear.
You do until the madness evaporates to a clear mind,
You do until physical pain eclipses the mental one,
You do until there is too much to take, until you come undone.
And everything stops for a while, your body and soul needing time,
This clawing, scorching anxiety now fades away,
But stays the fear, the dread, the wait, for when it sweeps you again.

Thoughts, Those Demons

In the dark, cold room that I'm stuck in, lying, sitting, standing still,
The thoughts trapped by daylight, by people and things and colors,
They are left without bars, without chains, running around and up the hill,
And they always are the darkest, the most violent, full of hatred and terrors.
Frozen in my cold dark room, I let their venom get to me, taint me again,
And I search, I imagine, all those unhealthy ways to cope with this pain,
That threatens to rot my insides, to melt my mind, to consume me whole,
And I think of scars, of blood, hazy minds, lost body, dried paper and alcohol.
Self-loathing, a gnawing need to claw at my skin, so raw, so brutal can rapture me,
And those demons... My thoughts... My voice... Wrap themselves so easily
Around a shaking body ruined by sobs, tainted by the tears of a bleeding soul.
My heart erected walls so tall those demons spill over less and less frequently,
But I know they aren't so far away, waiting for them, others, life, to push them over gleefully,
And I won't spill any more tears, any more torments over something out of my control.

My Beast

Releasing the beast inside, a perpetual growling beneath the surface
It's clawing its way from my guts to my throat, suffocating me
As I fight to keep it down, to keep it tamed – won't it just keep its place?
Won't it just stop clenching my heart as it fights to be let free?
What can I do? It has my eyes,
What can I do when I see my soul inside?
It's wild and brutal, my free spirit, unbridled beast,
Will it ever be sated of all needs, of all feasts?

Disguise

I used to wander on this earth on my own,
Weighed down by all this struggle boiling inside,
Smiling, laughing, so no one would have known
This pain, these gutted feelings that were some sort of pride.
This face in the mirror, this face the world could see
Was just another painting, another piece, a theatre
So they could hear all the lies they wanted to hear, I had to offer,
So they could live with who they wanted, who they needed me to be.
A ghost is what they saw, who they talked to,
A picture to hide a rotting core, a scorched soul.
Sometimes I wished they would finally notice
And see what was within, hidden; yet the world is selfish,
Too selfish to see what was simply is.
They asked, but they didn't want to know,
So I lied, again and again, to spare them the cold truth.
Deep down, did I ever want them to know?
To be exposed, vulnerable, I didn't trust them with my heart nude.
They kept turning a blind eye so their bubble wouldn't burst
When they could see in my eyes the sadness, the loneliness
That I came to cherish - at least they would always be there-
But if they searched, violated, known me, would I have shown trust?

Gangrene of The Soul

I hate myself for feeling like shit. Or hating myself makes me feel like shit,
But there's a part of me that's rotten, that wouldn't let me go,
Like gangrene corrupting every part of my soul, tearing it to bits,
And I don't fight, I never fight, 'cause it's me, it's me, and I fucking know.
I could walk like this forever, a hard numbness in my eyes seeing all grey,
A tension in my jaw to contain it all within, to keep me from going astray.
Before my distant gaze, tears prickle, sadness tickles, playing my heart
Like a broken instrument for a dissonant harmony, for wretched art.
It rains inside, so much that I feel it flooding, soaking dried-up walls,
I could punch my way through, scratching the stinking smoke off my skin.
Murder in my mind, death in my blood, it's the darkness that's making me stand tall,
And I keep going, my light darkening, as I walk surrounded by my sins.

Wrecked Boat

I'm a wrecked boat, stranded on a beach,
Wood all rottin', worn, torn sail flapping at the wind,
I'm all dried up, all dried up, giant breach,
The salt and the sand coating a once pristine brim.
Suffering the long decay of a thousand years, a thousand tears,
Here on this lonely shore, lovely bore,
Treasures lost on the way, stories whisked away,
Just left lying a broken skeleton, coffin all but wanton.

Shattered

Shattered in countless little pieces,
All scattered, all lost, buried, floating,
I won't be whole ever again, feeling
Broken, staggering, filled with uncertainties.
I walk in a world so distant, so cold, powerless,
Amongst a million faces with blank masks, lies.
I see in the broken glass a lot of tenderness
That I crave, deprived. I seek to die.
Time slowing to a stop or spiraling so fast
That I stumble and fall so many times,
Mixing the present, the future, and the past,
All this is worthless, a life for a few dimes.
I keep this wandering going till my feet bleed,
So that I could, for the first time, feel
A something that tugs at my insides, a sole
Something that could mend a broken soul.

Disillusions

Everything vanishes in a puff of smoke in the twilight hour,
All powerful during the day, I fall back to vulnerability,
And I wish I could keep forever more that much power
To sustain confidence, a strength... imagined it must be.
One second so sure in my boots, a solid heart,
And the next, everything shudders and cracks and stumbles
When all there is left are two words that I call art,
As everything else seems like a mad invention, so subtle.
And maybe thinking I could be so important is a crime in itself,
If so, my punishment is heavy on the soul,
And maybe thinking I am worth more than I am, more than a shell,
Is an illusion that keeps shattering, left dull.
My mind crawls, sinking in the moving sands of a world
That no longer hangs on my thoughts, on the poverty of my words.

Frazzled

Sometimes, it feels like wherever
I look, there is nothing for me there.
Maybe I travel just to run away some more,
Run as fast as I can until my whole body's sore.
My mind is often in fractals, shattered, frazzled
As if the world was too dull, not for me; I'm not dazzled.
I'm just floating in a perpetual unknown.
Please, may something stay before I'm too far gone?

Part of The Furniture

I feel so invisible and so empty,
Part of the furniture that you don't even see.
I don't belong anywhere; the world feels like a cemetery
Where I'm losing years and years,
Wandering around, trying to find my tomb.
I don't know what I'm looking for.
Does it matter that I matter?
Should I care if other skeletons want me around?
I keep wandering, wondering if I don't come from afar,
Unable to learn how to human properly,
A longing in me when I look up at the stars...
I'm not where I'm supposed to be.
I see bonds and connections all around me,
Spider web,
And I float next to it, unable to stick.
So I fly to the next.
Never a spider, forever a fly,
Invisible, annoying, always just buzzing.
Should I even try?

Shadow

A faithful companion, this one,
My shadow,
Always fuller at dawn,
Me? Hollow.
It drifts in the breeze, barely hanging on to me,
Like my thoughts – the irony.
Always elusive in the sunlight, so much so
That I could forget
How it unfurls all over me, even when I say no,
After the sun sets.
Primal watcher of my every move, I should embrace you fully.
Dark parts of me I shouldn't remove, let me see you wholly
And in a sacred breath, let's be one, once again,
Under the starlight or the pouring rain.

Coarse

No matter the scars, the bruises all over your body, your heart,
The battles, the fights, will not tear your soul apart,
Emotions rising and storming, riding tornadoes in the dark,
You bleed and scream, tears running down, wild and free; you're stark.
With each dusk comes a new funeral for a part of you that went its course,
With each dawn, you will see a new piece of you uncovered, a past life, a near future.
You might feel like a diamond in the rough, raw, invaluable, and coarse,
But you already brighten the world around of a shy light that grows and strengthens, insecure.
A soldier of the mind, a soldier of the heart, those battle wounds just as many memories
That shape you into who you are, hurt and strong, hungry for life, hungry for stories.
You shall rise among corpses of past hardships, ashes of your torments, your feelings
Floating around you, glowing embers reflected in your eyes, dancing.

Red District

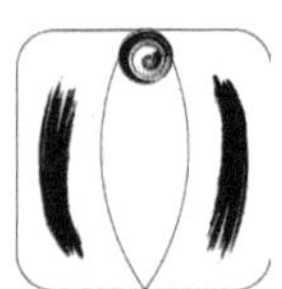

Apologia of "Fuck"

There is no word more beautiful than fuck,
No other word that gets you stuck, struck,
There is no better word that rhymes with duck,
No other as poetic as the great word fuck.
There is the powerful and angry fuck,
The one that gets ripped from your guts,
That makes you want to bleed the whole world dry,
That you wish you could scream in an enraged cry.
This one incinerates your whole soul to the ground as the world around you burns in the flames of fucking hell, damnation tearing you apart, and you can't fucking breathe, and you can't fucking scream, and you're tied down like a crazed animal in this small cage, and you fucking push out, you fucking growl and claw at the air, claw at the wall and lose your mind and FUCK!
There's the sad, the whispered fuck,
The one uttered in the loneliest hour of the night,
Because it's the only word that you can say right,
Your voice shaky, tears held back as your eyes are shut.
This one is the only companion to your aching heart, the one that's fucking shattering in a million of goddamn pieces and you don't even know why, you feel like shit, your thoughts are fucked up and dragging you in the fucking dark, and you see the fucking light but you can't, you won't, you wouldn't reach out because you fucking love the pain, you love the darkness so goddamn much because it's always there, this twisted friend, it's never going away, and you feel less alone and less damaged because the fucking pain whispers it's okay, whispers you don't deserve shit, you aren't worth shit, no one fucking loves you, no one fucking cares and.... fuck....
There's the sensual, sexual, moaned fuck,
The one that gets pulled out of you by this mighty need,
And this blazing desire that flows through you, awestruck,
Your core reduced to a throbbing soaked heat.
And it feels so fucking good to be taken, hard, deep; all you can hear is your groans, and you sound so needy, your hips bucking,

always wanting more, and your legs are wide open, pleading silently to be treated like a whore and you whine, you fucking whimper because all you feel are those fingers inside of you and your fucking body lives on its own, covered in sweat; you look like a fucking slut as you writhe and beg and shout; your body is on fire, you're fucking owned, but you don't give a shit because you're fucked harder, and you feel the pleasure building up, and it feels so fucking good, please harder, please, please don't fucking stop, right there, right fucking there, damn it, God, God, you're gonna..... FUUUCK!!
No better word to define the intensity of a feeling, of any feeling,
How could I express my love for this word that sounds so exquisite,
So expressive that you could be climaxing, enraging, or in despair sinking,
And yet this word would still be there, even for a flirt, even for wits.
Fuck.

Leading

Running through the wilds, without direction, it seems,
Pursuing some phantom dream that I can't foresee
With a heart thudding in my chest, bursting at the seams,
I flee so my mind is blank, just a void, empty.
But the occasional nymph would distract me from my path,
Leading me to a world of perdition, lust, and sin,
But my heart is a desperate lover, such is my epitaph,
Leading me astray as I let them all in.
I'll willingly succumb to the siren's call – my downfall,
But what a sweet death it is, your voice in my ears.
Why should I resist such a lewd yet alluring call,
When it takes me to sweeter waters than the salt of my tears?
Just a word, and I'll assume any position for you, please,
Just a look and I'll open for you, wanton or a tease,
Just a touch and I'll beg for you, desperate, clenching,
Lead me through the haze, for my submission is fleeting.

Extinct

You make every single one of my thoughts go extinct,
The way you approach me, the way we touch, is all instinct.
Under your piercing gaze, I'll gladly be your prey,
Be the goddess to whom, on my knees, I pray.
Unearthing deeply rooted desires that I had buried,
You tantalize the animal in me up to the surface,
Twisting my needs to your whims so I'd fold like a reed,
And all night long behave, obedient, at your service.
Apart from our feverish silhouettes forever intertwined,
Apart from our desperate breaths and sweaty skin,
Apart from our burning cores and longing hearts combined,
What else is there to existence?
Except for us both, it's only disappearance.
Loving you is but a dreamy omniscience.

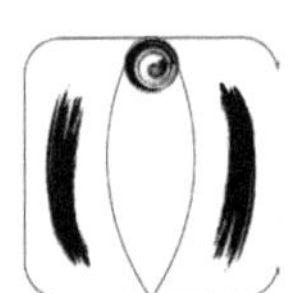

Slow

Take
It
Slow
As you peel every layer off my body – revealing
My breath itches for a beat, release – expecting
Why
Don't you
Pick up the pace, just what's needed, to leave me chasing
After you, as you chuckle above me, teasing.
I'm trying to hide it, but my thighs are parting – open book
I'm all lip bite and enticing eyes, under you – insidious hook
What
Are you
Waiting for, your prey squirming around, grabbing onto the sheets,
Wondering when you'll get her clenching and whimpering in defeat.
Hurry up, please, do not keep me yearning to feel all of you possessing me,
Your hands around my throat, my breasts, hips or entering me,
Take
It
Slow
When the time is right. It is, after all, not a chase but a treasure hunt,
So please, o please, just pound me senseless until all I can do is grunt.

Convert

Your breathy whispers in my ear chant psalms of a new religion
Made of what your words allude to, sins I hadn't envisioned,
Your rasped promises of divine experiences and sensations
Leave me breathless, holding onto you, trembling and wanton.
Convert me to your gods, please, bring me to your altar.
Let me worship the holy, depraved as I am, and taste thy nectar
As my trembling hands reach out to touch and grab onto anything,
Make of me what you want, your priestess, the one you're sacrificing.
Let me crawl, crazed, desperate for all your sung temptations,
And lay naked as an offering, I'll let it all go, complete abandon.
Punish me, if need be. My faith will withstand any flagellation.
Ruin me, damn me, pervert me, but please mark me with your passion,
So that in moments of respite, I can look and never forget
That I was weak enough to love you, to desire and convert.

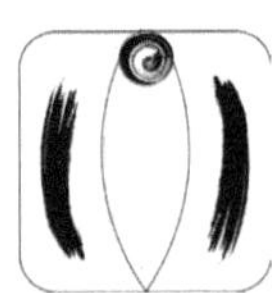

Livin' The Sub Life

Spending my time on my knees, 24/7
Makin' me crawl, promisin' me heaven,
I'd lick your boots, kiss the ground you walk on,
Just to do things that will turn you on.
Tie me up, real tight, so I can't move,
Grind on me, use me to your own groove.
Gag me so I can't talk,
Blindfold me so I can't walk,
A candle-lit dinner, use the wax, I'm the board to your chalk.
Restrain me, control me, shut me up, bondage,
I'll be yours, forever, 'till we die of old age.
And all these years, I never knew
Just how hard I could fall for you,
Make me yours, make me yours
I beg of you.

Exhibition

Put on display for your eyes alone, dear, an artwork in your exhibit,
More or less dressed, baby, you make me the expression of your whims.
Is there a better audience than your eyes, darling, doting, or strict?
I'm craving more, Mistress, don't leave me there, kneeling, it seems.
Bound and helpless, I'm waiting. Shoulders and knees sore, but I ain't moving.
Blind and gagged, I'm panting. Remaining senses heightened, ears are straining
To hear any sound you make, sniffing the air like a bitch for your scent.
But you just watch silently, dreaming of the picture you wanna paint.
But please, I'm begging, come to me, don't leave me blank – white canvas,
Mark my flesh with your passion, ownership, a masterpiece at your service,
Leave me trembling for the brush of your fingers on my sensitive skin,
I want you to dirty me; won't you brand me where they can't see – within?
How long will paint have to drip for you to put an end to my torment?
Am I meant to stay exposed, naked, horny, for your amusement?
Would you let others come and watch or sully this depraved exhibition?
Or will you keep to yourself and forever cherish my gift, this submission?

Worship

O me of so little faith, how do I atone for the sin
Of desiring you, Goddess, with such defiling thoughts?
Anointment with thy slick on my chin,
It's prickling the very flesh, mine, that you wrought.
How do I confess to you secrets I do not behold?
It's written on my face, shining in my eyes – the untold.
So I listen, dutifully, thy moans and grunts, my Gospel,
As I commune with you, drinking thy nectar like I'm under a spell.
You are power incarnate, Mistress, let me worship at thy feet.
Will you answer my prayers and save me from this heat?
I will be thy priestess, naked under the moonlight, if need be,
I'll offer you my whole self, if you wish, to honor thy sanctity.
Let me worship at thy altar, for I am a soul lost to you.
Let me leave the secular, for I am immortal for loving you.
Funny, isn't it, that the chains you hold around my neck
Are not blasphemous, but a lifeline from a wreck.
Let me worship all night till I bruise, on my knees,
For you look so holy, my dear, when you're pleased.

Contemplations

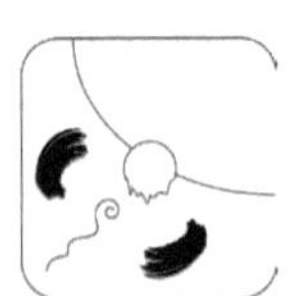

Hunger

There is something in me that calls
For something greater than the present.
It burns my soul 'till it becomes incandescent,
And leaves black smoke from my mind's coals.
I absorb the world inside like a sponge,
The ugly, the beauty, the holy, and indecent.
A hunger growing with no precedent,
That devours, scavenges, and I indulge.
The mundane numbs it down.
So, I keep my sanity in check,
But the mundane with you on deck
Keeps it aflame, won't let it drown.

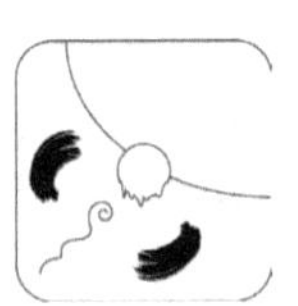

Dreams and Discoveries

This feels like a dream, a path to an abandoned manor
Where the leaves roll around in the deafening silence of an old splendor,
Ivy climbing the façade just like you around my heart,
Feelings wandering and losing themselves in this maze, this work of art.
In this home of a thousand memories, a thousand lives,
Fingers gliding on old wood, breathing thousands of secrets,
I lose myself to those ghosts, those flickering stories
While you become somehow tangible, more real than all those lies.
And all those treasures, hidden in every room,
Couldn't be as precious as the ones you keep inside,
As I cherish every glimpse, every whisper of an insight.
If this very manor was to be our impending doom,
I want you to know, to understand, that every hour
Which comes to pass embellishes this world, ours.

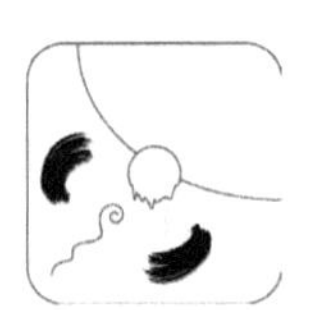

Green Roses

There is a field, out in the meadow, by the little river everyone knows.
It's ignored, full of weed, they say, not worth another look, another thought.
But they didn't come close enough to marvel in wonder at what I saw:
A field of green roses, where I found a treasure I didn't know I sought.
Some flowers are torn, shriveled, too exposed to the burning sun, to the wind,
Some flowers didn't blossom yet, resting in the shade of others, afraid of being,
Some flowers are gorgeous, resplendent, glowing with life and mystery
But all of them, those unknown green roses, they are all perfect to me.
My fingers might be itching to pick them, to bring them home for myself,
But I much prefer walking to the field every day and staring in contemplation
Of a life that I could have disregarded and put aside, like an old book on a shelf.

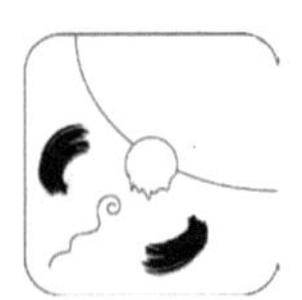

Standpoint

Feeling like Icarus, my dreams wings too heavy to fly me to the sun,
So many roads in front of me, all appealing, all within reason,
Yet I stand still, wrapping bandages around my bloodied feet,
The road behind so long, rocky, made beautiful by victories and defeats.

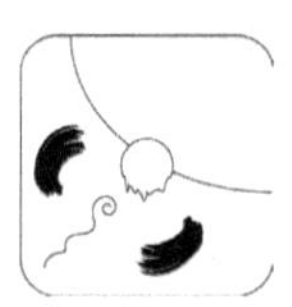

Who Knows

Who knows what people hide
When they lie with a beautiful smile,
Who knows what is deep inside,
Who whispers what is worthwhile.

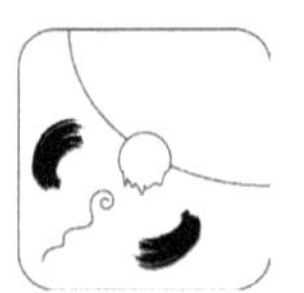

On Stage

Unexpected emotions – a shaky voice, a shaky breath –
As you reach inside, letting the lyrics roll out;
The audience disappears, everything fades to black
But the music around you, but the feelings inside.
Meaning for others to be touched – deep within, where it's held tight –,
You reach where there's only yourself, without walls, without artifice.
It struck a chord, vulnerability pulled out, tears not meant to be yours;
You're taken by the moment as they watch your emotion pour.
It rings too true, too much like your inner voice, that you forget to act.
But the beauty resides where it can gut you and rip you apart,
When your heart isn't guarded like it should be, when you let yourself be.
When art stops imitating to embody life, when words and music can be
The mirror, no, the sight of all your insecurities and dreams,
Then you stand on the stage, singing, diving in, and forgetting to breathe.

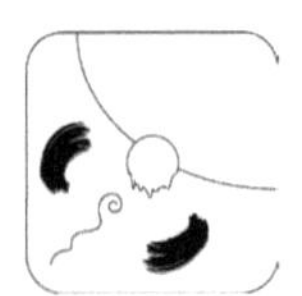

Freedom of Doubt

In my line of questioning about freedom, I fear
That all I can see is just an illusion, an ideal,
But where do I begin? Freedom for the body, the mind, the soul?
All those thoughts turning like an infinite wheel.
Freedom of the body seems so impossible,
Restrained by gravity, physics, and it's incredible
How the sheer limit of our abilities is a prison for body expression,
And yet my hands glide on the paper; I don't feel imprisoned.
My past and my present collide in this physical shell,
This body that I can move freely; I feel free,
Just can't do everything I want it to;
Disillusion, awareness; I am not free.
Thoughts dictated by emotions, memories, lessons I was taught,
Thoughts I expressed that are mine, I feel free,
Too much fog, too many parasites, can my mind really just be?
Mind weakening the body that weakens me, battles I haven't sought.
But isn't all this living for my soul?
A breath of life, a spark of infinity; I feel free,
But I know my soul is restrained by my mind, trying to control it,
Trying to guide it towards a perception of happiness, I am not free.
And I am afraid, I feel empty when I think of this.
I will never be free; I can't even free myself from my own being,
Let alone from other's pressure, from society, from expectations.
I let hate take over me; I am not free.
Not free from what they want me to be, from what they expect of me.
Not free from the violence around me that paralyzes me; I do not feel safe.
Not free from the hate I have for this violence, disrespect, idiocy.
Not free from my own fears for a future I know nothing about, for death.

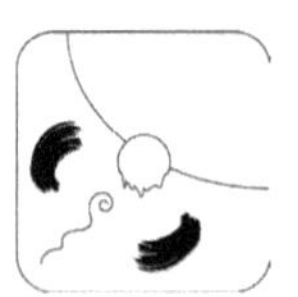

And yet I feel free. Maybe am I?
What if freedom isn't doing whatever you want?
What if freedom is taking responsibility, living my humanity peacefully;
What if freedom is staying honest with me and with others?
It's being brave; to be free is to be brave.
No one will give you this freedom: you have to fight for it.
Freedom is having the same chances as anyone else to be who you are,
To live in happiness, with dignity and respect.
This freedom I feel privileged to have, I cherish;
The freedom to doubt and learn, the freedom to grow.
The freedom to offer my thoughts to the world,
The freedom to just be, to live, to love.

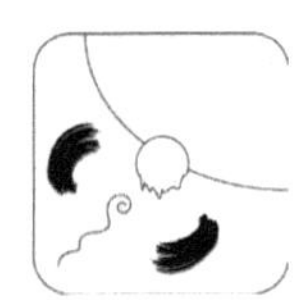

Subconscious Space

Open-eyed but still so blind, reality is a morning mist,
Countless lives, countless memories, like a call from the outside,
Creating worlds so vast, a lore so deep, life of an artist,
Just the need of your hand, of my name from the other side.
An eerie forest, pale sunlight shining through, like an oneiric painting,
Every step on the ground, every breath of the cold morning air, a thought,
Every bird singing, echoing, a cry from the past, alone in a sensory drought,
Everybody is just one, every tear, every battle wound, a mind that's bleeding.
A flutter, a twitch of fingers, another little sign of hope,
Your voice forever near, forever here, a lifeline, the most solid rope,
Holding on through unconsciousness, subconscious space, an anchor.
Learning about beyond, listening to what seems to be a whisper carried by the wind,
There is within more to discover, to care for, to love, the beggars and the king,
For too long cast aside, for too long ignored, faced when the shell is held in stupor.

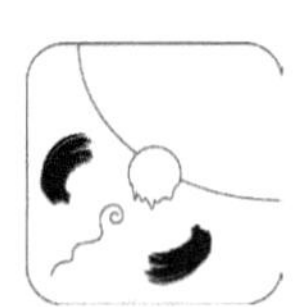

Forever Companion

I've searched for you in various places, in so many faces,
Thinking you would be the one I would share my life with,
But what I was searching for was a place away from myself
Because it was too hard to see the woman I am and will always be with,
Hard to look at all she was and still find a way to love, to embrace.
I dream of another woman by my side; is it to distract myself from me?
Someone I could shower with love and affection that I don't give myself,
Thinking that I don't deserve, that I'm not enough, too flawed, too perfect.
And finding yourself is hard, trying to know when you're trying to hide,
Chasing an illusion, an imperfect mirror, realizing you hate the one inside.
In loneliness you suffocate because she's here, even in darkness,
May you be awake, may you travel through your dreams, madness.
It's so fucking easy to be tired, so exhausted of who you are,
Because it's so brutally honest, and ugly, and too true, too real;
So you cage yourself away in fear, the bars made of ideals.
Your soul runs free, wild, destroying everything to get to you,
And you stare, helpless, in pain, slowly dying, hungry, angry,
Until, if it ever does, the cage slowly fades away like shedding skin,
And you may find yourself holding onto a desperate soul, a tight embrace, soothing.

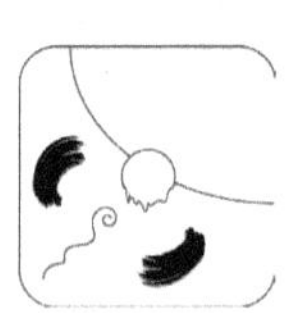

A New Definition

I used to believe love to be those burning fires, those raging feelings, and torments,
I used to believe it was all about those scorched lovers, bloodied and full of scars,
That it was poems ripped right from the heart, shouted at the moon, at the stars,
And restless nights, daydreams, a head full of desires; a full life now turned crescent.
But with you, I know it's about the secret smiles from wordless gazes,
I know it's also tender touches just to know you are here, a fleeting always.
Your arms around me, a warm embrace, like a summer sun, a Sunday morning,
And those dreams, your vision, your thoughts, all whispered but so inspiring.
The poet in me will keep being transcended by this otherworldly passion,
Sparked by the warmth you bathe my heart in, by the love in your eyes.
She will still wish to lay down words, so devastating, enraptured, chained,
Like savage wolves howling at the night sun, tearing apart all that I am, destruction,
To honor, to tell the tales of the simplicity, the ease, the serenity that inspires
The woman I love so wholly, so holy, sharing a feeling so pure it can't be claimed.

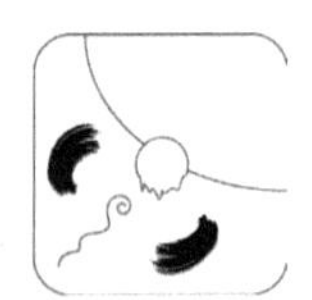

Consequence

O the delicate balance of actions and consequences...
How am I supposed to live this life in the trenches?
Carefully plan out each step so as not to
Step on a foot of a fool who's on the lookout too?
Is life about caring about any possible outcome
As you desperately hustle for a meager income?
Or should it be to take a leap of faith and dive,
Taking a risk for a life for which you're willing to strive?
Now, I know, I know, we should care as to not hurt another,
We should care for and respect the life of all,
But as long as I remain harmless, can I be bold?
Can I close my eyes and fall, always faster,
Towards an uncertain future, towards my dreams?
Walk along paths of swaying flowers and falling leaves?

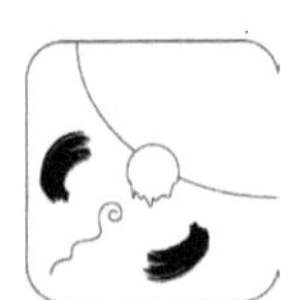

Drift

There are times when things are just adrift
And all I can do is watch things float away,
Rarely are things in life a brutal shift,
It just bubbles and spills – thoughts kept at bay.
Is there better than floating in the sea
With one's ears underwater, eyes to the skies,
Dreaming of the world and all the different lives
That go on around and without lil' old me?
There's comfort in a moment of nothingness
As the world keeps on turning,
It gives its worth to the harrowing emptiness
That's sometimes still lingering.

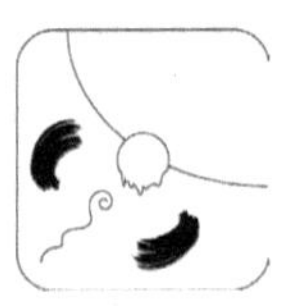

Purpose

Should we be driven by purpose every second of the day?
Is there any meaning to me looking into art on display?
Is there power in a mundane movement of my finger in the air
To affect the world in an unknowable future – a blessing or a scare?
It is exhausting to give purpose to every little thing I do.
So what if I just want to exist, rest my mind for a second or two?
It is exhausting trying to come up with willpower I do not have
When I just want to experience an existence I cannot halve.
Good or bad, useful or useless, what's the matter of it all?
Will it help me get back up if I stumble and fall?
Happiness is not the destination but the journey, they say,
No purpose needed, let me be lazy on the way.

Nothing Left to Do

I'm sitting here not knowing what to say,
The whole world on the tip of my tongue, my fingers sitting on letters.
I stare at a white page, searching in the darkness of my mind,
But somehow, I lost the key to my (he)art.
Sometimes words just flow out incessantly on the page, all meaningless,
But when so many feelings fight to be expressed, there's this blankness
That I wish I could fight and burry in the ground,
Useless corpse, no more sound.
What is there left for me to do?
What magic could I bring into this world
Without words, without thought?
What is there left to do?
How to move forward and put a foot in front of the other?
If there's nothing left to do, then I'll just be,
And I'll think of you sitting next to me.

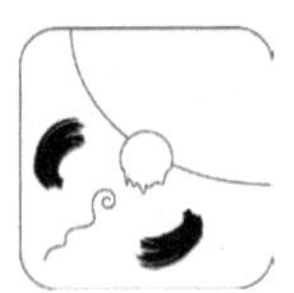

Setting

Wood cracking under my feet, heart thumping,
I close my eyes, obscured by a heavy curtain.
Voices ushering all around and inside, maddening,
I repeat those words, this desperate prayer, uncertain.
There's a sunset behind me that gives no light,
Cracked paint,
There's an audience before me, hidden in plain sight,
Horrid taint.
A curtain call for all to see –my hungry witnesses,
A stage to my mad folly –rising deafening voices,
A gaze I can never escape –all eyes on me, all eyes on me.
It rises as a golden light, beckoning and O so sweet,
Take me, take me, O listen to my pleas!
Let me, on this hereby stage, fall to my knees,
Welcome to my demise so that my self I can finally meet.

Utterance

Every word should be uttered with a meaning,
Because careless words are set free and roam the skies as fallen stars,
Shining to looks of regrets,
Dancing in the air as fireflies and latching onto every heavy silence,
And only regret remembers what was left unsaid.

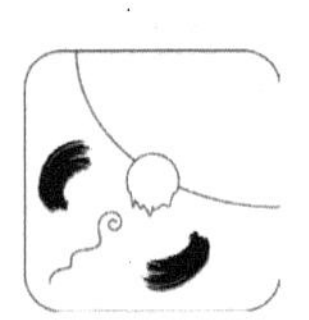

Silence

Silence is an infinite that we rarely ever reach,
Sounds always ringing to fill it as it is never left alone.
The air vibrates in a never-ending melody.
If not from something else, your breath,
Your own existence will make a sound, loud.
But the silence inside is just as hard to reach.
When the silence around you starts peeking through,
It's only to reveal the ruckus inside, the torrent of thoughts.
It's all jumbled and always so noisy, like static.
Sometimes you may slow it down to a near stillness, but...
Is there ever the absolute absence?
Or is life always pulsing on a perpetual beat?

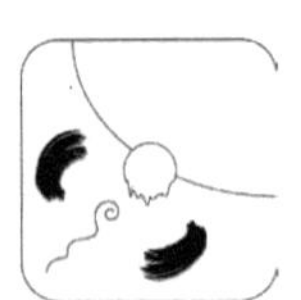

Permanent

Everything changes around me, constantly,
And to be fair, so do I.
Why do I keep grasping for a sense of security?
I don't know why.
It just ebbs and flows, the universe, without pressure,
Like water, it adapts and carries on,
Forever moving, the only thing I know for sure,
Knowing more than it lets on.
Don't expect your life to go against that principle,
My dear self, my dear ego.
Why should people stay by your side, identical?
It is natural to let them go.
What is immutable, though, is that it all is One,
Through time, space, and lives.
So take it all in, the absolute, the moon and the sun,
For nothing ever dies.

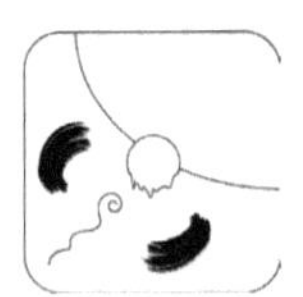

Time

I can feel it, when I'm happy, the sands of time escaping my grasp,
Its softness cascading through my fingers, no matter how tight the clasp.
So fleeting, I try to chase it so it may slow down, for just a moment,
It's futile, I know, but what else am I to do, so despondent?
How I wish I could travel this dimension like I do the other three...
To be able to go back in time to moments when I'm most free,
For the only times I'm aware of time existing – shhh, it's a secret,
Is when I'm sat, contemplating a way to stop being its puppet.
For when a smile stops time and engraves itself in my heart,
I know it'll dissolve over time in my memory;
See, that's why I always try to capture life in all of my art,
Because time is naught but treachery.

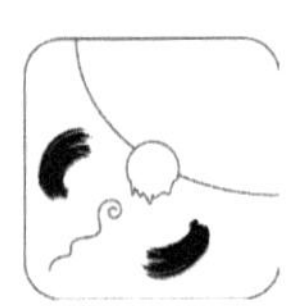

Compassion

Why am I this harsh with myself, always demanding more?
Why does taking care of myself sometimes feel like a chore?
I should treat you, me, with more tender love and care;
When you're afraid, I should become your teddy bear.
I should laugh and cuddle you, inner me, as childhood besties;
I should talk you down from somber thoughts to see your smile.
But, instead, I abandon you to demons, all things dark and vile
When I should hold you gently until everything simply empties.
Let me smile at you through rainy days, myself, and you'll see
That you're happier and stronger than you believe yourself to be.

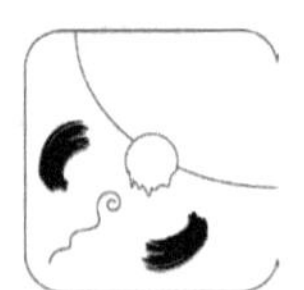

Moon-Touched

We are walking together, shoulder to shoulder
In landscapes enveloped in the cloak of the night,
Looking up at the moon as we go without a word
Through a ghostly dream revealed in moonlight.
From so far away, she watches over us all and reveals
Some invisible beings and superposed otherworldly realms.
As moonlight reflects sunlight, she's at the helm
Of a reflection of the world, pragmatic layers peeled.
Shadowy doubles a fraction too slow
Give beings this spectral glow,
While unseen-before creatures prosper,
Unveiled to our eyes in shimmering silver.
Moon-touched, us all, voyeurs of primal mysteries,
Soul-touched, us all, seers of untold stories,
Let us for a little while yet walk among you,
Before you disappear until the next moonrise is due.

Weave

Everything has its thread out here in the universe,
And I tug on all of them,
So they wrap around my fingers.
In a golden light, I stand, feverish,
Weaving and weaving stories after stories.
Sweat on my skin, muscles spasming,
I maintain my crazed tango,
And tangle lifelines and lifetimes
So that we can keep meeting.
To our love, no embargo,
To our destiny, no shrine.
Across this ever-expanding tapestry, Universe,
I'll lay down your very foundations,
So that my mind cannot disperse
As my words sing in utter adoration.

THE END

About the author

Born in France, Del Thoreau spent most of her twenties traveling. When she wasn't busy being a physiotherapist, she pursued her passion of storytelling. Despite loving its many forms —music, photography, or cinematography— it is words that make her the happiest. After fifteen years of writing for herself, she has finally released her first collection of poems: Soul Shards.

www.ingramcontent.com/pod-product-compliance
Lightning Source LLC
LaVergne TN
LVHW091315150826
845673LV00006B/1657

9782959025624